NIGHTS AT THE CIRCUS

NIGHTS AT THE CIRCUS

by Tom Morris and Emma Rice

adapted from the novel by Angela Carter

OBERON BOOKS
LONDON

First published in this adaptation in 2006 by Oberon Books Ltd
521 Caledonian Road, London N7 9RH
Tel: +44 (0) 20 7607 3637 / Fax: +44 (0) 20 7607 3629
e-mail: info@oberonbooks.com
www.oberonbooks.com

A catalogue record for this book is available from the British Library.

ISBN: 978-1-84002-631-3

Cover image: Keith Pattison

Visit www.oberonbooks.com to read more about all our books and to buy them. You will also find features, author interviews and news of any author events, and you can sign up for e-newsletters so that you're always first to hear about our new releases.

A NOTE ON THE TEXT

Much of this text was inspired by the improvisations of Ed Woodall, Andy Williams, Nat Tena, Mike Shepherd, Amanda Lawrence, Carl Grose, David Glass, Gísli Örn Gardarsson, Stu Barker and Adjoa Andoh, without whom it could not have happened and to whose theatre-making craft it is dedicated.

Tom Morris and Emma Rice

Characters

VESTA

JACK WALSER

THE CREATURES OF THE THEATRE

THE WINDJAMMER

FEVVERS

LIZZIE

MA NELSON

MR SUGAR

COLONEL KEARNEY

THE STRONG MAN (SAMSON)

THE PRINCESS

THE CLOWN (BUFFO)

MIGNON

This adaptation of *Nights at the Circus* was first performed on 20 January 2006 at the Lyric Hammersmith, produced by Lyric Hammersmith and Bristol Old Vic in association with Kneehigh Theatre, with the following cast (in alphabetical order):

Adjoa Andoh, VESTA, THE PRINCESS

Stu Barker, THE WINDJAMMER / MUSICIAN

Gísli Örn Gardarsson, JACK WALSER

Carl Grose, LIZZIE, SAMSON

Amanda Lawrence, MA NELSON, MIGNON

Natalia Tena, FEVVERS

Andy Williams, MR SUGAR, COLONEL KEARNEY

Ed Woodall, BUFFO

THE CREATURES OF THE THEATRE and other parts were played by members of the company

Director Emma Rice

Designers Bill Mitchell and Vicki Mortimer

Lighting Designer Malcolm Rippeth

Music Composition Stu Barker

Sound Design Gregory Clarke

Costumes Lyric Wardrobe

Additional Costumes Keith Watson, Mark Costello and
                      Kay Coveney

Wings Ivo Coveney

ACT ONE

VOICE-OVER: Ladies and Gentlemen, please turn off your telephones and other electronic appliances and prepare to travel in time. Because Europe is agape for the end of the century. Not this century. Or the last one. For we are at the fag-end, the smouldering cigar-butt, of a nineteenth century which is just about to be ground out in the ash-tray of history.

We are in London and it is 1899.

VESTA enters. She is dressed immaculately in men's clothing, top hat, tails and a cane. The WINDJAMMER (musician) is onstage throughout.

VESTA: By the water
      I was walking
      When I heard a step

      My woman stood there
      By the water
      This is what she said

      Die, old century die
      Give us the chance to let yesterday lie
      Die old century die
      We haven't lived yet and the moon is high

      Honey don't you
      Hug and kiss me
      Don't you hold me tight

      All for cash I
      Sold my body
      I'm not yours tonight

      She said Die, old century die (*Etc.*)

JACK WALSER, sitting in the auditorium, scribbles in his book.

JACK: End of the century. Obviously a woman but dressed as a man. Seems to be talking in the voice of man. Doesn't quite make sense. Seen better in Reykjavik.

A finger sticks out through the curtains and points at him. At first he ignores it. Then he reacts. The finger beckons him onto the stage. He goes onto the stage.

Finger points out through curtains. Seems to be telling someone off. Audience laugh. Points at the audience. Seems to be pointing at someone. Seems to be pointing at the person next to me. (*Ad lib.*)

The finger summons him onto the stage, then punches him. A CHORUS of Creatures of the Theatre enters and picks on him.

CHORUS: What the hell is this? A notebook and pencil? Does the man have no idea at all?

Did nobody ever tell you that bringing a pencil into a theatre is the worst thing you can ever ever ever do?

It's worse than bringing a pencil into your hotel bedroom on your wedding night.

IT COMPLETELY MISUNDERSTANDS THE NATURE OF THE EVENT.

What's in your notebook? No, don't answer that. I'll look. Ha! Haha! New York Times it says!

And Walser. Walser? What's that?

JACK: It's my name. Jack Walser.

CHORUS: And what's this language? It's in gibberish?

JACK: I'm originally from Iceland.

CHORUS: Oh! A Nordic Adventurer. (*Etc.*)

JACK: Who are you?

CHORUS: We are the creatures of the theatre. Nothing in this room can happen without us.

Look! 'Great Fakes and Con-artists of the World': A series of articles to blast out falsehood with the certainty of the coming century.

JACK: I see you read Icelandic.

CHORUS: A little.

One –

I don't believe it.

The greatest fake in theatrical history – the Winged Woman of London.

Do you have no experience of life at all?

JACK: I promise you, I'm no stranger to illusion. I've seen a child shin up a rope in the Calcutta market and then vanish clean away. In Kathmandu I saw a fakir on a bed of nails soar up until he was level with the painted demons on the eaves of the wooden houses.

The Creatures are struck with wonder.

Mass hysteria and the delusion of crowds. A little primitive techonology and a big dose of the will to believe.

CHORUS: You bitter hearted man! GET OUT!

VESTA opens the curtains, revealing FEVVERS, who sings her song. The CHORUS and JACK stay and watch.

FEVVERS: I am only a bird in a gilded cage
    With a lock that is copper and steel

Like a secret to last till the death of the age
With no one to touch and to feel.

CHORUS: She is only a bird in a gilded cage
With a lock that is copper and steel
Like a secret to last till the death of the age
With no one to touch and to feel.

FEVVERS: If I sing my song
Perhaps I'll find
An ear to hear
What I've got in mind
And I've got such a lot
In front and behind.

CHORUS dance as they sing.

CHORUS: She is only a bird in a gilded cage
With a lock that is copper and steel
Like a secret to last till the death of the age
With no one to touch and to feel.

FEVVERS: I am only a girl in a gilded cage
With a lock that was made to be broken
My secrets might die with the death of the age
But my secrets were made to be spoken

Oh death!
Oh death!
You're ever as close
As my next breath

Oh breath!
Oh breath!
You're carrying me
To my next death

If I sing my song
Perhaps I'll find
An ear to hear
What I've got in mind

And I've got such a lot
In front and behind.

As you look up at me with your sparkling eyes
All dewy and soft as the sea
Is there magic at work? Is it truth? Is it lies?
No, it's sweet indivisible me.

Curtains shut.

VESTA: Are you still here?

JACK: Well, yes.

VESTA: Got you interested has she?

JACK: No. I'm just writing my story. Your winged woman has arms as well as wings, right?

VESTA: Of course

JACK: Well the wings of the birds are nothing more than the forelegs – the arms. The skeleton of a wing shows elbows, wrists and fingers, all complete. A fabulous bird woman – if such a thing existed – ought to possess no arms at all. Her arms should be her wings.

VESTA: She's in there in her dressing room. Knock on the door.

JACK: It's a curtain.

VESTA: Try it.

He knocks.

The curtains open to reveal FEVVERS, crouched on the piano and feeding herself like an animal. WALSER looks at her, amazed.

FEVVERS: What's the matter? Ain't you never seen a girl eating before?

VESTA: Jack Walser had survived the Plague in Setzuan,
a nine week sand blizzard in Morocco, a sharp dose of
buggery in a Bedouin tent beside the Damascus road,
yet underneath he remained the same dauntless lad who
used to haunt the wharf in Reykjavik hungrily eyeing the
tangled sails upon the water until at last he, too, went off
with the tide towards the endless promise of New York.
He lived his wild life in a bubble of detachment. It was
as if he had never been touched by anything.

FEVVERS: Jellied eel. Want some?

JACK: No thank you. I'm Jack Walser.

FEVVERS: Call me Fevvers.

Enter LIZZIE, suddenly.

LIZZIE: You! Keep your hands to yourself.

JACK: Who are you?

LIZZIE: I'm Lizzie. I look after Miss Fevvers. And that's all
you need to know.

She frisks him.

He's clean.

Now sit down and don't move a hair in your nose until
she's finished her talking.

I know what you want. And you're not going to get it.

The clock strikes twelve with comical speed.

JACK: Is it midnight already?

FEVVERS: The light of day first shone down upon me
right here in smokey old London! I ain't billed the
Cockney Venus for nothing. Though they could just
have well have called me Helen of ruddy Troy – cos
just like the great Greek beauty I never docked by the

14

normal channels – oh dear me no – I was hatched out of a bloody great egg!

JACK: An egg?

FEVVERS: A touch of sham?

JACK: No thank you.

FEVVERS: Wet 'is whistle, dear Lizzie, and tell him where you found me all covered in egg shell and yolk and nesty bits.

LIZZIE: On the doorstep of Ma Nelson's brothel in Wapping.

JACK: A brothel?

LIZZIE: In Wapping. Ma Nelson's brothel in Wapping.

FEVVERS: Ma Nelson was our ship's captain.

MA NELSON appears.

LIZZIE: She always carried a sword. It's proper Spanish steel, not a copy, and it went with the uniform.

She flourishes her sword.

MA NELSON: For Protection.

Come on ladies of my academy. Let's show a bit of belly!

Enter the CHORUS of Whores. They dance.

Now ladies, up to the library for your politics lesson with Lizzie. All members of my academy must prepare themselves for the wider world. A clean muff is nothing without a clever head telling it which way to point.

FEVVERS: She had a lovely library. This old geyser left it her on account of the way she shaved her pubes. There was tarts in there with more book learning than you've got pimples.

LIZZIE: Right girls. Today it's gender politics. Here is woman. And here is man. And here is a today's lesson.

> Men deserve humiliation
> They are built for shame
> Custom made for degredation
> Born to suffer pain.
>
> When they are about to kiss you
> Crush them in the rocks
> If they say that they will miss you
> Piss into their socks

MA NELSON enters carrying LIZZIE's bag.

MA NELSON: Our Liz, all this will never do! You'll make us all redundant if you go on.

LIZZIE: It's just something I find helpful to hum while entertaining the clients.

JACK: Great. A revolutionary whorehouse. I wish I had been there, Miss Fevvers. But I'm writing about you.

FEVVERS: Not in a hurry are you Mr Nordic Adventurer? You sit here next to me.

WALSER gets up and sits next to FEVVERS.

You should know that there's no point in painting the angel without the landscape. You wouldn't know where it was macking flying, now would you? Stop thinking about the destination and you'll have more fun on the journey.

CHORUS: What's that?

MA NELSON: It's a bag. I found it on our very own doorstep.

CHORUS: What's in it?

LIZZIE: Look it's a baby.

CHORUS: All covered in egg shell and yolk and nesty bits.

What sort is it?

LIZZIE: It's a girl.

CHORUS: Good. Let's keep her.

Hang on. What's that on her shoulders?

Fevvers. Fevvers. Fevvers.

Let's give er a bath.

LIZZIE: (*Grabbing the bag.*) I'll have that.

FEVVERS: I didn't have one mother. I had a bevy of them. Speaking of which...

She offers him champagne.

Put hairs on your chest.

JACK: I've got hairs on my chest already, ma'am.

FEVVERS: Can't have us girls getting pissed on our own-some.

They make him drink.

Look at me, Jack. All titties in front and wings behind.

LIZZIE: You can see perfectly well from over there.

JACK: I'm only doing as I'm told.

LIZZIE slaps him.

FEVVERS: You wouldn't believe it, but I was a late developer. Flat as a board in front and behind until I was fourteen. But then I was plagued by a terrible itching between my shoulder-blades which made me rub my back against the furniture like a cat.

LIZZIE, giving FEVVERS a bath, sees the wings coming out of her back.

LIZZIE: Oh lawd. Oh lawd. Help! Ma Nelson. I think she's...got wings.

MA NELSON: It seems we have been entertaining an angel unawares.

LIZZIE: It is the annunciation of my menopause.

MA NELSON: Right girls. I'm pleased to announce the retirement of the worst whore who ever read book. From now on you'll look after Fevvers.

LIZZIE: And I have done ever since and will do till the world is blown to bits.

FEVVERS: It was the birds that taught me how to fly. There was a pigeon nest on the pediment outside our attic window and I saw how the mother pigeon taught her babies to totter along the edge of the wall. She would flap at them and they would flap back with an action not unlike a human swimmer. Then – one bright June morning – one of the chicklets was dithering on the brink, when its loving mother came right up behind it and shoved it clean off the edge.

LIZZIE: So I says, Fevvers, this might be the day of days. It was midsummer night, the year's green hinge.

CHORUS: Fly out of your pants
     Fevvers
     Fevvers fly
     Fly for all of us
     Embrace the wind
     Embrace the wind
     For all of us

FEVVERS: The business of the house was over. The last
cab had rolled away with the last customer too poor to
stay the night and all behind the drawn curtains were
at long last sleeping. Even those thieves, cut throats and
night prowlers who stalked the mean streets around us
had gone to their beds. It seemed a hush of expectation
filled the city, that all was waiting in an exquisite tension
of silence for some unparalleled event.

CHORUS: Leap out of your skin
     Fevvers
     Fevvers leap
     Leap for all of us
     Embrace the wind
     For all of us

LIZZIE: Although it was a chilly night she had not a stitch
on her so as not to impede the lively movement of her
body. Imagine that.

We crawled out onto the tiles and the little wind that
lives in high places came and prowled around the
chimneys; it was soft, cool weather and my pretty one
came out in goose bumps, didn't you, such shivering.

FEVVERS: Now it came to it, I was seized with a great
fear – and not only fear that the morning might find me
lying like a bag of broken bone in Ma Nelson's garden.
Mingled with the simple fear of physical harm, there
was a strange terror in my bosom that made me cling to
Lizzie's skirts. What would happen if I could really fly?

I feared a wound not of the body but of the soul, an
irreconcilable division between myself and the rest of
humankind. I feared the proof of my own singularity.

LIZZIE: So I did like a good mother pigeon and shoved her
off the edge.

CHORUS: Fly into the dawn
        Fevvers
        Fevvers fly
        Fevvers fly
        Fly for all of us
        Embrace the wind
        Embrace the wind
        For all of us

        Run wild through the sky
        Fevvers
        Fevvers run wild
        Fevvers run wild
        Run wild for all of us
        Embrace the wind
        Embrace the wind
        For all of us

FEVVERS: But right in the middle of the swim of it, I felt a
    pain in one of my wings. Then both. Cramp!

    What if, like the greedy girl in a fairy story, I'd bitten off
    more than I could chew and my first flight would be my
    last.

LIZZIE: Come on my love! Paddle.

FEVVERS: I smashed back in through the window arse up
    and legs spread like honey on a cake.

    Ma Nelson threw such a party to celebrate my flying.

MA NELSON: Crack open the rum! Maestro please!

    They dance.

MR SUGAR: Hello.

    You're like a little Cupid aren't you.

    Would you like a diamond?

JACK: Who is that?

LIZZIE: Mr Sugar. I wish she'd forget about him.

MR SUGAR: I have diamonds so clear you want to cut
your tongue on them, so big they make you shit, so
expensive that thinking about them gives you a damp
patch on your back.

Sometimes I look at my diamonds until I'm sick.

FEVVERS: What do you want for your diamonds?

MR SUGAR: I collect wings. I've got every kind of wing
in my house. Butterfly wings, bat's wings, finches wings,
flies' wings. Eagle wings. Crow's wings. Dragonfly wings.

I'd give a very very good price for yours.

MA NELSON: Get out of my house.

MR SUGAR: What do you say, Cupid?

I've got one diamond that's as big as a whelk. It's yours
if you say the word.

FEVVERS: Get away from me.

MR SUGAR: I'm a patient man. I've watched you growing
up. I know which is your room. I'll wait till you change
your mind. Which you will.

Exit.

JACK: Are you alright?

MA NELSON: Emergency meeting.

> Fevvers is not for sale
> She shall not sell her body as we do
> She shall work only for display
> She shall bring pleasure
> To the eye and to the imagination
> Not to the bodies of men

CHORUS: Not to the bodies of men

MA NELSON: Fevvers is not for sale
She shall be dressed as the Winged Victory
Posing as a statue in our parlour
And overseeing our trade.

She will be powdered white with chalk
Her hair tied in a ribbon
And as a symbol of her freedom
From the trade of this house
She will carry my sword.

CHORUS: She will carry Ma Nelson's sword.

MA NELSON: Which I now present to you Fevvers
Our Winged Victory
You are the pure child of the century
The New Age in which no woman will be bound to
the ground.

ALL: By any means necessary, we will be free. Amen.

Clock strikes midnight again.

JACK: What have you done to that clock?

LIZZIE: We could have stayed forever in that little heaven
on the Wapping High Street.

FEVVERS: But it was not to be. Ma Nelson met her end
with terrible suddenness. She was on her way to Blooms
to treat us all to salt beef sandwiches

MA says 'See you later' to the ladies of the Academy.

when she slipped on some foreign matter

LIZZIE: skin of a fruit or turd of a dog

FEVVERS: and fell beneath the oncoming hooves and
wheels of a brewer's drey and was mangled to a pulp in
a trice.

LIZZIE: Dead on arrival at the London hospital. No chance for even so much as a kiss me hardy.

And dear Ma Nelson had died intestate so the old place was inherited by her brother, a gospel grinder would you believe, who flung us out on the street without a penny.

FEVVERS: What are we going to do Lizzie?

LIZZIE: Nature has made you a spectacle people will pay good money to see. And all you can do to earn a living is make a show of yourself. You're doomed to that.

CHORUS: One last look at the old place.

LIZZIE: Let's remember Ma Nelson. The necessity that first united us – the universal need for cash, nosh and a roof over our heads – must now drive us apart. But the invisible bonds of our sisterhood will always knit us wherever we roam.

By any means necessary…

CHORUS: …we will be free. Amen.

They light their fags.

LIZZIE: I'll miss the place.

CHORUS: We all will.

LIZZIE: I'm sorry. I'm not myself today

FEVVERS: Fags away girls.

They throw them.

LIZZIE: and I seem to have spilt an awful lot of kerosene on the way out.

The brothel burns. JACK tries to put the fire out.

JACK: Help! Fire! (*Etc.*)

The fire goes out. JACK looks at the WINDJAMMER (musician).

JACK: Did you see that fire?

WINDJAMMER: No.

JACK: What about the smoke?

WINDJAMMER: No.

Enter FEVVERS and LIZZIE.

FEVVERS: And it's only a short hop from there to here, so to speak Mr Walser.

JACK: What do mean? Is that it?

FEVVERS: I've conquered the music halls and cabarets of Europe. Now I'm off to conquer the world with Colonel Kearney's Circus.

JACK: Colonel Kearney? You didn't say anything about the circus.

FEVVERS: Which is why if you want to find out any more, you'll have to talk to me in St Petersburg!

JACK: In Russia?

FEVVERS: Now me and Liz must get home to bed.

JACK: Can I help you find a cab?

FEVVERS: Gracious no! Waste good money on a cab? We always walk home after the show. Goodbye Mr Walser. It's been a pleasure.

LIZZIE: Don't be fooled; he's hard as a raw potato. No heart to him.

FEVVERS: He's like a piece of music composed for one instrument and played on another.

LIZZIE: More like an unhatched egg.

FEVVERS: Goodnight Mr Walser.

They leave. He makes as if to follow them.

JACK: Wait.

Curtains close behind them, leaving the playhouse creatures looking at JACK and VESTA.

My watch says it's still midnight. How did they do that?

VESTA: Did you get your story?

JACK: Yes. No. I'm not sure.

VESTA: Losing your touch?

JACK: No. I don't think so. Smoke and mirrors isn't it? Where are you going?

VESTA: To the circus.

JACK: Wait.

Maybe I need to be refreshed – need to have my sense of wonder polished up again. It's the ambition of every red-blooded kid to run away with the circus.

VESTA: As a clown?

She puts white paint on his face as she sings.

So I asked her
If I kill you
Will it set you free?

Can't we find
A new tomorrow?
She said back to me

There's a strange face
In my mirror
One I've never seen

Did you think that
Paint and grease could
Make you feel so clean?

Die old century die.

ACT TWO

FIRST MOVEMENT: COLONEL KEARNEY'S CIRCUS

The curtains close on CHORUS and immediately there is a drum roll. COLONEL KEARNEY bounds onto the stage.

KEARNEY: Howdee St Petersburg!

Welcome! WELCOME! WELCOME! to the greatest show this side of the twentieth century.

You think you've laughed before.
I'm telling you. You've never laughed before.
You think you've cried before.
I'm telling you. You've never cried before.
You think you've seen a circus before?
I'm telling you. You ain't never seen a circus before!

You're going to laugh tonight St Petersburg.
You're going to cry to tonight St Petersburg.
You're going to see a circus tonight!
Because this is the greatest show this side of the twentieth century!

And who I ask is the brain behind this, the greatest show this side of the twentieth century?

What magician? What patrician? What logician? What mathematician? Who is the GOVERNING GENIUS behind everything you're seeing tonight?

No madam. Don't look at me. I am not worthy to touch the hem of her garment. Ladies and Gentlemen, please put your hands together for the brains and the beauty behind this outfit…

Enter SYBIL, the mystic pig.

They say that behind every successful man is a superfine intelligent lady. Well in my case she's a nine year old Kansas white spot pig called Sybil.

Don't you want to roll her in chocolate and call her a truffle?

But she ain't just a pretty face. She's all mind.

She's got a business mind.
She's got a creative mind.
And she's got a psychic mind.
And there ain't nobody gonna put so much as an inch of air between me and my pig.

Let me tell you a little bit about me and my pig.

> Me and my pig are the finest combination
> Me and my hawg are the hottest team you'll find
> You'll see that my pig has the psychic divination
> You'll see that my hawg has a perspicacious mind
>
> Me and my pig, me and my pig, me and my pig,
>   me and my pig.
>
> It was a long time ago
> Down in Lexington Kentucky
> The day I got lucky
> With a pig
>
> I was hooking school
> And I saw a pig and bought her
> And I took her home and taught her
> How to jig
>
> Me and my pig, me and my pig, me and my pig,
>   me and my pig.

With a talent like that, it was no surprise when she turned out to be PSYCHIC. She's got a twitch and when she gets a twitch, I get an itch. And that means she's spotted a SHOWBUSINESS OPPORTUNITY.

From the smallest seeds
You can build yourself an empire
And my small seed
Was a pig.

Cos the pig came home
One night with a juggler
And a dwarf with a carrot
Coloured wig.

And that was how our circus began.

Me and my pig, me and my pig, me and my pig,
    me and my pig.

Now let's see whether Sybil can sniff out any talent in
this house tonight.

JACK: Excuse me sir. I'd like to join the circus.

KEARNEY: I'm sorry. Sybil says you have no talent at all.

JACK: I'd like to be a clown.

KEARNEY: Sybil says you're not funny.

JACK: I'll do it for no money if you like.

KEARNEY: Sybil says it's a deal.

You'll be a jam face – that's what we call a new clown
– and you'll do whatever anyone in the circus tells you.
At all times.

And these are the people who will be ordering you
about.

*Curtains open to reveal the circus ensemble, STRONG MAN,
PRINCESS and CLOWN.*

STRONG MAN: I am the Samson. I am from the Europe.
Look at my muscle. Look at me! I am lovely.

KEARNEY: He's not the brightest man in the circus but his penis is the size of a pole cat.

STRONG MAN: Yes it is.

KEARNEY: Buffo. I've got a new jam face for you. No talent, no experience and no wages.

BUFFO: Great.

KEARNEY: Your bonus

Gives him bottle.

He's been top of the bill for seven years.

BUFFO: I'll top the bill for you, colonel, till I die.

I'm only funny when I'm drunk.

KEARNEY: And this is the princess of Abyssinia.

JACK: How do you do? I'm Jack Walser the new Jam Face.

KEARNEY: Stay back.

She didn't grow up or suck milk in the human world, no sirree, she was found and fostered by these very tigers in the Abyssinian jungle – she grew up speaking their language in return for which one of her adopted brothers bit out her tongue, since when she hasn't spoken a human word.

JACK: What's she doing with that gun?

COLONEL: She turns her back on the tigers in the act. She puts herself at their mercy and seduces them with music.

STRONG MAN: Her back is covered from butt to neck with scars – like a jig-saw puzzle.

BUFFO: No one goes near her that isn't covered in fur.

Enter FEVVERS.

FEVVERS: How about a few fevvers then darling?

KEARNEY: And here's my new star signing. It's Fevvers, the Cockney Venus herself!

FEVVERS: Hello Russia.

BUFFO: Oh yes. A freak act come to steal our applause.

STRONG MAN: I am the Samson. If you are lucky maybe one day we make jumpy jumpy together.

FEVVERS: Well, well, well, Jack Walser. So you've run away to join the circus, have you love? That shows a bit of stick. I'm impressed.

JACK: Yes. I'm going to be a clown.

FEVVERS: Well, you can't have everything.

KEARNEY: I see you know each other. How charming. Now if you'll excuse us.

FEVVERS: That's right colonel. Let's go and put some detail into my contract.

KEARNEY: Walk this way.

KEARNEY and FEVVERS negotiate the details of her contract during a tango. As they negotiate, LIZZIE rewrites the contract, resting on the back of the pig. He agrees to give her the following:

FEVVERS:

- A thousand dollars a month paid directly into my account in Ireland
- the bridal Suite in the Hotel Europe in every town we stay in
- no rehearsals
- an arranged tour of the libraries and museums in each city we visit, for me and Lizzie

- a case of French Champagne and a full pound weight of Belgian chocolate for the opening show in each town

- jellied eels, mash and bacon shipped weekly from Fosters in Wapping

- I will be top of the bill for the whole tour

- I will have always have my own carriage to carry me from the hotel to the circus

- anchovy paste and a new badger hair shaving brush every month for Lizzie.

The curtain closes. LIZZIE still has the pig.

LIZZIE: While your muff-struck master is sleeping, you enjoy your freedom my duck. Here. Have a chocolate. I'll take you out in the yard and you can run around wherever you like.

There is the sound of beating. A curtain opens to reveal BUFFO with MIGNON.

BUFFO: It's alright. She's my woman. Let me tell you what a lucky girl she is.

> I was sitting in a café
> With a monkey at my side
> When I saw a pretty waitress
> With a ribbon in her hair
>
> She seemed to like the monkey
> And she sat with us a while
> So I took her home
> And showed her how to care
>
> Now she's my woman
> She's the old clown's woman
> And even when I beat her she is mine
> Everybody knows she is the old clown's woman
> And I beat her yes I beat her all the time

As we walked through the streets
She was crying like a child
But she handed me the ribbon
She was wearing in her hair

And she told me of a time
When she was young and she was happy,
She was skipping with her sister
In the square.

Her mother did the washing
And earned money from the soldiers
And her father would come home
To make the fire and cut the bread

But on one sunny day
Daddy couldn't find the breadknife
So he went outside to look
For it he said.

Now she's my woman
She's the old clown's woman
And even when I beat her she is mine.
Everybody knows she is the old clown's woman
And I beat her yes I beat her all the time.

As her father went outside
With the breadknife in his pocket
He was thinking of the soldiers
In the town and what they'd said

About the sweet pretty lady
Who came up to do the washing
And how easily she lay down
On the bed.

So he waited by the pond
With the knife. And he killed her.
And he drowned himself.
The reeds were in the water round his head.

And the poor little girl
Had no father and no mother
And no money and no breadknife
And no bread.

She's my woman
She's the old clown's woman
And even when I beat her she is mine.
Everybody knows she is the old clown's woman
And I beat her yes I beat her all the time.

ACT TWO: SECOND MOVEMENT: LIZZIE, JACK AND THE TIGER

LIZZIE enters in commando fashion and fiddles with the bomb she is building in her bag.

Curtain opens to reveal FEVVERS on trapeze, humming. WALSER enters.

FEVVERS: Since you've followed me all the way to St Petersburg. Why don't you follow me up here?

JACK: I'll stay on the ground thank you. I'm here to write a story about you…about the circus.

FEVVERS: Suit yourself.

LIZZIE enters.

LIZZIE: Eh. What you want?

JACK: I'm going to be a clown.

LIZZIE: You! I don't believe it.

JACK: I'm joining the circus.

LIZZIE: You learn nothing. You listen nothing. You make problems. You don't go away.

She destroys his notebook.

You won't be needing that.

OK. I help you.

JACK: Thank you.

LIZZIE: Let me see.

Underscoring this, FEVVERS is singing.

FEVVERS: Men deserve humiliation
    They are built for shame
    Custom made for degradation
    Born to suffer pain.

    When they are about to kiss you
    Crush them in the rocks
    When they say that they will miss you
    Piss into their socks
    Piss into their socks

    With women they say
    To be cruel is to be kind
    With men it's enough to be cruel

    I've the wings of a swan
    And the heart of a lion
    And I'm buggered if I'm anybody's fool.

    Come on all you lady-chasers
    Come on all you wags
    You will feel pathetic
    As you queue up for your shags

    Men deserve humiliation
    They are built for shame
    Custom made for degradation
    Born to suffer pain
    Born to suffer pain.

    She is the death of dong
    And never get her wrong.

She is the courage drinker, the stinker.
Listen to my song
She will take away your prong.
She is the pinky shrinker, the thinker.

LIZZIE: You can't have these clothes. I'll help you find better ones.

She strips him.

Don't move. I'll be back as soon as I've sold these.

I know what you want. And you're not going to get it.

Leaving him half naked, she goes off. MIGNON enters and looks at WALSER.

JACK: Hello. I'm the new clown.

She lifts her skirt. JACK turns away. STRONG MAN enters. She lifts her skirt to him. They have sex. A curtain is drawn over them. LIZZIE returns with WALSER's clown costume. She finds him looking into her bag. She punishes him further.

LIZZIE: Never ever ever ever look inside a lady's hand bag.

LIZZIE goes off. WALSER tries to learn some tumbling. STRONG MAN and MIGNON are revealed, still having sex.

The pig comes screaming across the stage. Then KEARNEY.

KEARNEY: Tiger out! Tiger out! Bright as fire and dangerous as death, with the stink of half rotten meat pouring out of it with every breath.

A tiger enters.

Everyone freezes.

STRONG MAN: Don't eat me, tiger. Please. I am the Samson.

STRONG MAN leaves.

MIGNON tries to put her pants on, trips and screams.

The tiger goes for MIGNON. In the same moment JACK goes for the tiger.

The tiger mauls JACK.

PRINCESS enters with the hose and squirts the tiger off.

JACK and MIGNON are left in a heap.

FEVVERS: What's all this ruddy racket?

LIZZIE: Nothing. Ah my little Fevvers. Just a little tiger mauling.

FEVVERS: Who?

LIZZIE: No one important. It's just the Nordic adventurer. I think he's alive. Charged a bleeding tigress, apparently. What the 'ell got into him.

FEVVERS: Where is he?

They enter the space together and see JACK but not MIGNON.

Ooh. That's proper chewed up.

LIZZIE: Charging a bleedin' tigress? What the 'ell got into you?

FEVVERS: Let's ave a look at you.

WALSER gets up revealing MIGNON, who runs out holding what clothes she can.

What?

LIZZIE: Quick work. I only left him for a minute.

FEVVERS: Who's she?

LIZZIE: The Clown's missus. She's a pin cushion.

FEVVERS: I can see that.

LIZZIE: You've got a ruddy cheek, you have. Making all soft Icelandic eyes at Miss Fevvers in your interviewing and then THIS!

JACK: What? What do you mean?

FEVVERS: Lizzie. Give me a rag.

JACK: I was just changing my clothes.

FEVVERS sticks the rag in his mouth.

FEVVERS: Bite on this. That involve screwing the Clown's missus, does it? Alcohol.

She pours alcohol on his back and leaves him on the floor.

BUFFO enters.

BUFFO: Hello Jam Face. You in pain? Don't worry I'll take you down to clown alley.

ACT TWO: THIRD MOVEMENT: THE CHURCH OF THE ACHING SIDES

BUFFO is cradling WALSER. Around them, a chorus of clowns.

BUFFO: Let me tell you a story.

I was in Copenhagen when I had the news of the death of my adored mother, by telegram, the very morning on which I buried my dearly beloved wife who had passed away whilst bringing stillborn into the world the only son that ever sprang from my loins.

All my loved ones…dead.

But that afternoon at matinee time at the Tivoli, I dragged myself into the ring and tumbled and fell – how they roared with delight.

And then – in a moment – I looked up at all the grinning faces and I froze…like a baby gasping for air. And they laughed.

'I can't go on!' I screamed at them. 'My heart is broken!' And they still laughed. And I drank in their laughter.

After the show, I scrubbed off my clown's face and staggered to a bar in the thickest part of the town. And I drank and I drank until I didn't know who I was.

I wanted to drink in the entire world and piss it out against a wall.

And a barmaid turned to me and said, 'It can't be that bad.' 'Oh but it is,' I said. Then she gave me some advice. 'Take yourself along to the Tivoli this evening. Have a look at Buffo the Clown. He'll put a smile on your face,' she said. 'He'll put a smile on your face.'

Scrape off these faces and what do you find?

Despair. Failure. And Pain.

The crowds laugh at our failure. They love our humiliation. The greater the humiliation, the greater the clown.

That is why we are top of the bill, my friends. That is how we keep the circus alive. They love our pain. And our pain redeems them.

So you see a clown is like Jesus looking forward with bright eyes to his martyrdom.

But as they sit there in heaven, do they laugh when he falls? Would we laugh if we got there too?

> The clown is the image of Christ
> Despised and rejected of men
> They have broken the bones of his body
> In order that they feel alright.

Oh do they laugh in heaven or do they not?
Or will it just be milk
And tricycles
And tubs of cream
And liquorice and silk?

Oh do they laugh in heaven or do they not?
Or will it just be smiles
And pointy feet
And flower beds
For miles and miles?

His shoulders are stooped by the fury of the mob
His closest friends betray him as the cock crows.

Oh do they laugh in heaven or do they not?
Or will it all be toys
And butterscotch
And rubber balls
That flash and make a noise?

Or will it just be nightingales
And mattresses
And breath
And handsome men
With silver flutes
That smell a bit of death?

Will they laugh as he suffers and bleeds?
Will they laugh as he hangs upon the cross?

Do they laugh in heaven or do they not?
Or will it just be pipes
And bottletops
And paper hats
And racing cars
With stripes?

Or will it be a pool of light,
A pretty pair of shins,

A sugar horse,
A spray of rain,
A box of copper pins?

Come on then, new boy.

He looks into JACK's face.

Now what do we see here? A chicken. I see a chicken.

In the name of Christ the clown, I christen you Flappy
the Chicken.

*The clowns put on the rest of his costume, making him look
like a chicken.*

Go on. Flap like a chicken. Say cock-a-doodle-do.

BUFFO puts JACK's hat on.

This is to stop you hearing your brains as they trickle
out.

Welcome to Clown Alley

He kisses him. MIGNON enters.

MIGNON: Walser. Mr Jack. I never forget what you done.

BUFFO won't look at her. He looks at his clowns.

BUFFO: What's she talking about?

*BUFFO gets the message that JACK has had sex with
MIGNON. He signals to the clowns to restrain WALSER.
They do. He beats up MIGNON. JACK is horrified. He shouts
to stop it. BUFFO beats up WALSER. The clowns leave.*

VESTA: Then at last
My woman kissed me
We'll be free she said.

Maybe in
The coming century
When this one is dead.

Die, old century die
Give us the chance to let yesterday lie
Die old century die
We haven't lived yet and the moon is high

WALSER wakes up and sees MIGNON. He picks her up. They stand, naked, like Adam and Eve.

JACK: I'll take you somewhere safe

ACT TWO: FOURTH MOVEMENT: THE COLD CREAM, THE GIRL AND THE BATH

MR SUGAR stalks the foyer of Fevvers' hotel. FEVVERS and LIZZIE enter. He is carrying flowers.

MR SUGAR: Hello Cupid. Remember me?

FEVVERS: I've give you my answer already.

MR SUGAR: Please yourself.

FEVVERS: But I'll have these.

Nonetheless, she accepts the flowers, but MR SUGAR doesn't let go of them.

MR SUGAR: In exchange for your picture.

FEVVERS: I haven't got a picture.

MR SUGAR takes out a camera and snaps her.

MR SUGAR: I have.

I've got a little bit of you and I'll be coming back for more.

Enter JACK and MIGNON.

FEVVERS: You are pushing your luck right out of the harbour, clown boy!

LIZZIE joins in wherever possible.

I quite like stupidity in a man – but you really gild
the lily, you do. Show up here dressed like a chicken
because surprise surprise you've got nowhere to keep
her. Well sort your own effing mess out! And stop
following me round like a King Charles Fucking Spaniel.

JACK: Fevvers. Do you ever shut up? Look at her.

JACK hands MIGNON to FEVVERS.

Her skin is mauvish, greenish, yellowish from beatings.
Fresh bruises on fading bruises on faded bruises. It is
as if she has been beaten flat, had all the pile, the shine
banged off her adolescent skin. Or as if she has been
beaten to the thinness of beaten metal.

FEVVERS: Take her, dear Liz.

*Gently LIZZIE takes MIGNON off towards the bath. She
gives her a box of chocolates.*

Don't think you're off the hook.

JACK: It isn't how it looks.

FEVVERS: You're not going anywhere. What the cocking
hell is she going to think of you? The least you can do is
see how she scrubs up. Follow me.

LIZZIE: Look at you, you little pigeon, like a bag of
spanners. What's your name, love?

MIGNON: Mignon.

LIZZIE: Lovely. Mignon. Well let's see what Lizzie's got
in her bag for you Mignon. There is only one cure
for a beating like that. Chocolate and a Warm Bath.
There you are. That's right. That one's a cherry cream.
Come the revolution we won't have to put up with
any of this shit. Don't you worry. We'll clean you up
and set you up so's you can earn money and look after
yourself. Fevvers'll probably try and fix you up in the

performance line of things, but I'd give my eye teeth to get you a nice steady job in an ice cream parlour or a brassworks or something respectable like that. By any means possible, we will be free, Amen.

MIGNON is in the bath by now and she sings:

MIGNON: So we'll go no more a roving
      So late into the night
      Though the heart be still as loving
      And the moon shine still as bright

      For the sword outwears the sheath
      And the heart outwears the breast
      And love itself must cease
      And the heart itself take rest

      Though the night be made for loving
      And the day return too soon
      Yet I'll go no more a roving
      By the light of the moon.

FEVVERS and JACK find themselves pulled irresistibly into contact like two drops of mercury. Then they separate.

FEVVERS: Come 'ere. Kneel, Mr Walser. Closer.

She removes his make-up.

Make you pretty.

I hate clowns. I truly think they are a crime against humanity. Gawd, the poor girl! Out of Clown Alley and into the arms of the Nordic Adventurer. Talk about the frying pan and the fire!

MIGNON is sitting on LIZZIE's knee being cuddled.

Up on your feet and sweep her off hers. They've put me in the bridal suite, as you'd expect, but you can have it for the night.

LIZZIE: Laugh! You'll be the death of me! Don't look at me that way, Viking boy. If it was up to me we'd keep the pretty one and chuck you in the cocking river.

FEVVERS: Come on Lizzie. She sings like a little canary and I've got an idea about how she can make a bob or two of her own.

LIZZIE: If he says that he will miss you...piss into his socks.

FEVVERS: Look at me. Play nicely.

MIGNON offers herself to WALSER. He half-heartedly makes an advance but hurts his arm (or something) and loses interest. MIGNON falls asleep with her face in the chocolates.

WALSER creeps out of bed, leaving MIGNON with a flower. On his way, he is ambushed by the STRONG MAN.

STRONG MAN: I'm sorry. I have to do this.

JACK: Do what?

STRONG MAN: I am the Samson. You took my woman.

JACK: What woman?

STRONG MAN: The Mignon.

JACK: But she was the clown's woman. I already got beaten by the clown. There's no need.

STRONG MAN: She was my woman really. I am the Samson.

JACK: You know nothing happened between us.

STRONG MAN: I can't be sure.

JACK: Don't be stupid, of course you can.

STRONG MAN: People are saying the dirty things. I'm sorry my friend. It's a matter of the honour.

JACK: But I couldn't have been anywhere near her
– because she had her ankles round your neck.

STRONG MAN: Do not say the dirty thing. Do not
impugn my the honour. The shame is too great. I am the
Samson.

Never before have you had such a fisting. No hard
feelings.

ACT TWO: FIFTH MOVEMENT: THE LAND WHERE THE LEMON TREES GROW

FEVVERS finds MIGNON. She is alone.

FEVVERS: Where is Jack?

MIGNON: Gone.

FEVVERS: What about your night in the bridal suite?

MIGNON: Nothing.

MIGNON shakes her head.

*LIZZIE arrives. FEVVERS and LIZZIE get MIGNON
dressed.*

FEVVERS: The cruel sex threw her away like a soiled glove.

LIZZIE: But us girls ave gone and sent her to the cleaners.

FEVVERS: From today, you'll be earning your own
money.

They dance her off to the tiger cage.

A nightingale, Princess, a birdy for your beasts.

PRINCESS signals not to speak.

Just cos they don't like speaking doesn't mean they won't
like singing. Music makes words heavenly, dunnit?

One little listen won't hurt you. She's called Mignon.

LIZZIE: Don't worry little flower. That's a loaded gun on her pianna and she ain't afraid to use it.

MIGNON: Do you know of the land
      Where the lemon trees grow?
      Do you know
      Sweet sister
      My friend?

      Do you know of the land
      Where the animals sing?
      Do you know
      Sweet sister
      My friend?

      For might not this land
      Be the old land of Eden
      Where time was lost in the seas?
      Where innocent beasts
      Play among the wise children
      All safely beneath lemon trees?

FEVVERS: Well there's a lovely chance. Ruddy great instinct I've got, isn't it Lizzie? Big as a barge.

JACK: That's beautiful, Mignon. That's beautiful.

LIZZIE: It's your beau. The Nordic adventurer. Back for more Nordic adventuring no doubt.

FEVVERS: How's the wonky arm?

JACK: OK I think.

FEVVERS: You take care of it. Scratch of a tiger can fester something rotten, that can. And don't worry. I know you walked out on our little canary last night, after all. Seems like I got it wrong, poppet. Seems like you weren't knocking her off, after all.

JACK: No.

FEVVERS: Well it doesn't look like she'll be pulling your bell any more either.

JACK: I promise you. She never did pull my bell.

FEVVERS: I must say, Mr Walser, it's very flattering you should pursue me thus, to the ends of the earth, you might say. Eh?

LIZZIE: I know what he's after. And he's not going to get it.

LIZZIE looks into her bag and does some work on her bomb. The PRINCESS gets MIGNON to dance with the tiger. The other tiger gets jealous.

MIGNON: Yes I know of the land
　　　　Where the lemon trees grow.
　　　　Yes I know
　　　　Sweet sister
　　　　My friend.

　　　　Yes I know of the land
　　　　Where the animals sing.
　　　　Yes I know
　　　　Sweet sister
　　　　My friend.

Hummed chorus during which the following dialogue happens.

LIZZIE: Ooh look. The lady tiger's getting jealous and the princess wants a volunteer to dance with her. Off ye go, young feller and do your duty for Colonel Kearney's Circus!

FEVVERS: I say, ain't that a bit much?

LIZZIE: No. It's fine. Ain't you the Nordic Adventurer? Where's your spirit?

JACK: But that's the cat that tried to eat me!

FEVVERS: E's a wounded soldier poor sod –

JACK: – my arm

LIZZIE shoves him into the cage.

LIZZIE: Now we'll see what he's made of.

WALSER and the lady tiger join the dance. The new act works.

CHORUS: Oh let it be the land
Where the lemon trees grow.
Let it be
Sweet sister
My friend!
For I come from the land
Where the birds cut the sky
With their wings
My sister
My friend.

ACT TWO: SIXTH MOVEMENT: A TRICKY NIGHT AT THE CIRCUS

KEARNEY enters to announce the circus. As he tries to enter, BUFFO is audible arguing with him.

BUFFO: I made your fucking circus. And now you're topping the bill with a freak act.

KEARNEY: You're drunk.

Ladies and Gentlemen. The greatest show this side of the twentieth century will tonight perform for the last time ever. Why? Because it's new year's eve 1899 and tomorrow we won't be the greatest show this side of the twentieth century WE WILL BE THE GREATEST SHOW OF THE TWENTIETH CENTURY! And to mark this MAGNIFICENT occasion we have a new star to top the bill tonight, The Cockney Venus, Fevvers….

Fanfare. KEARNEY turns upstage to face an imaginary audience on the upstage side of the ring door curtains.

But first on tonight – a wholly new feature – it has music, danger, romance – The Princess of Abyssinia, her Ferocious Tigers – and singing in the jaws of death without any protection the Lovely Mignon.

The ring door curtains close behind KEARNEY.

We are are in the ring door area, the 'backstage' of the circus ring.

BUFFO enters, climbs the ladder and tries to cut the trapeze rope with a knife. SAMSON helps him.

BUFFO: Top of the bill. I'll give you top of the bill… (*Etc.*)

STRONG MAN: You are so funny my friend Buffo (*Etc.*)

JACK WALSER enters and sees BUFFO up the trapeze.

BUFFO: Where is your face, clown boy?

JACK: What are you doing?

BUFFO: I baptised you. I kissed you. Put your fucking face on.

JACK: I'm not a clown any more.

BUFFO: It's not your job to decide whether you are a clown or not. Who do you think you are? I am Buffo!

JACK: The colonel has put me in the tiger act.

KEARNEY: (*Offstage.*) And now ladies and gentlemen, please welcome the waltzing tigerboy from the land of ice.

JACK: I'm on.

BUFFO: You're clowning tonight my boy, colonel or no colonel. But before you put your face on, and before you do your clowning, I'm going to beat you to death.

JACK: But why? I haven't done anything.

STRONG MAN: I love your manly chat, but I think they are ready for you, ice boy.

BUFFO: What? You fuck my woman. And then I have to watch you giggling like a pansy with the bird woman – with a fucking freak act – while she takes my place at the top of the bill! Not done anything!

STRONG MAN: It's getting dangerous out there. The lady tiger is so very jealous.

JACK: I have to go out there. They're starting the dance. They can't do it without me. It isn't safe for Mignon.

KEARNEY: (*Off.*) Tiger boy!

STRONG MAN: The tiger is approaching. Mignon's back is turned.

BUFFO: What the fuck do you care about Mignon!

A gunshot from behind the ring door curtains. The curtains are parted and we see the tiger, dead, PRINCESS holding the gun, MIGNON distraught.

The PRINCESS drops the gun and goes to comfort MIGNON. BUFFO picks up the gun.

As the ring door curtains close on the nature mort, KEARNEY enters, breathless, looking for WALSER.

KEARNEY: Where in the Sam Hell were you? You're fired, you hear? But before you're fired get out there and move that dead tiger!

WALSER and KEARNEY exit through the ring door curtains upstage.

BUFFO picks up the Princess's gun and gives it to STRONG MAN.

BUFFO: Samson. I want you to help me. Imagine we've got a huge audience in front of us. And I say to you 'Please my friend shoot me.'

STRONG MAN: Heh heh you are brilliant. (*Etc.*) Hello imaginary audience. I am the Sampson. I am from the Europe. Hello. (*Etc.*)

BUFFO: Here. In the leg. Yes. Go on.

SAMSON shoots BUFFO in the leg.

Aaaaaaaaaargh! It's agony. You fool! What are you doing? No. It's ok. It's ok. Now do it again.

STRONG MAN: Really? Do it again? You are brilliant.

BUFFO: Yes. Really. Here. In the side. (*Etc.*)

SAMSON shoots BUFFO in the side.

Aaaaaaaargh! (*Etc.*) How could you do that to me? (*Etc.*) Please. One more. In the head. Please.

STRONG MAN: Very good for comedy. The rule of three. Ha ha.

He shoots him again. BUFFO dies.

KEARNEY, clearly audible from behind the ring door curtains, announces:

KEARNEY: Please welcome ladies and gentlemen, the high chief of chuckling, Buffo the Clown.

Curtains open to reveal BUFFO dead, STRONG MAN holding a gun.

KEARNEY closes the curtains in horror.

What did I do to deserve this today?

JACK enters.

JACK: I got rid of the dead tiger.

KEARNEY: Now get rid of the dead clown.

JACK drags BUFFO's corpse off the stage.

OK Samson. Get out there and save the show!

Curtains open. STRONG MAN goes through the curtains, which close. Crowd boos.

KEARNEY: Oh shit.

I'm sorry Sybil. I know you don't like her but she's our only hope. Fevvers! Fevvers! I need you out there now!

FEVVERS enters.

FEVVERS: Double my fee.

KEARNEY: I quadruple your fee.

Curtains open. STRONG MAN comes off.

STRONG MAN: It's not going very well out there.

KEARNEY goes off through the curtains.

KEARNEY: (*Off.*) Ladies and Gentlemen, please stay in your seats. It's the Cockney Venus. Fevvers.

The curtains start to open.

JACK returns to see what's happening.

JACK: No. Fevvers. It's not safe. The trapeze. It's not safe. (*Ad lib under song.*)

FEVVERS: Get off the stage.

> I am only a bird in a gilded cage
> With a lock that is copper and steel
> Like a secret to last till the death of the age
> With no one to touch and to feel.

> If I sing my song
> Perhaps I'll find
> An ear to hear
> What I've got in mind
> And I've got such a lot
> In front and behind.

The trapeze breaks. She hangs there.

JACK: Wait there.

JACK graps the rope and twizzles her round. The curtains close to huge applause. They have saved the show.

Not bad, eh?

FEVVERS: You haven't understood a cocking thing, have you, clown boy?

JACK: We saved the show.

FEVVERS: Don't you ever step inside my limelight again.

JACK: Don't be stupid, Fevvers. I was helping you.

FEVVERS: I don't want to be in a double act. I want to be free.

JACK: I don't believe it Fevvers. You misunderstand everything. You misunderstand everything about me. I didn't have sex with Mignon. I'm not following you around like a King Charles Fucking Spaniel. I am not trying to steal your limelight. I'm trying to do my job.

FEVVERS: What do you think it looks like, with me spinning round and round and you standing at the bottom like a hero from the cock-shoving Edda. I haven't slogged my tits off to become the top of the bill in order for you to waltz up and fiddle me about like a puppet on a straffing string.

And did it never occur to you Mr Nordic Adventurer, that the reason people misunderstand you is that like every vain and cowardly cock-chafing man since time immemorial, you never ever ever say what you actually want.

Now fuck off back to Clown Alley.

He does. She collapses, exhausted.

LIZZIE approaches her.

LIZZIE: There you are my little chick. All safe now. It seems your fancy boy is not quite the man he seemed.

Well as you know, personally I've never been in favour.

Well shot of him, I say.

FEVVERS: Why did you adopt me, you miserable old witch? I was free when you found me. No parents, no nothing. Then you clapped eyes on me and I was your thing, Ma Nelson's thing, everbody's thing. Sometimes I reckon I'd have been better off being nobody's thing. God I feel sick.

LIZZIE: I don't begrudge you my company, darling. We must all make do with what rags of love we can find – flapping on the scarecrow of humanity.

FEVVERS: I don't want your company. I don't want anybody's company. I don't want anything. No people. No circus. No wings. Go!

She goes. FEVVERS is collapsed.

By any means necessary I will be free. Amen.

Enter MR SUGAR.

Jack?

MR SUGAR: Hello Cupid.

I've come for your wings.

I have watched you for a long time.

Night after night after night at the circus.

I have a picture of you in my pocket.

And a diamond for you in my hand.

I have a house in every pretty city in Europe.

I have diamonds so big they'll make you shit.

Don't worry.

Just have a little drink.

FEVVERS: Yes sir. I like a little drink.

She takes a sip. It is very strong. He drinks a lot with no effect.

He starts to feel her wings.

What are you doing? What are you doing?

MR SUGAR: I'll give you all the diamonds you could dream of.

FEVVERS: Don't. I –

MR SUGAR: All I ask is that when you go, you give these to me.

I'll give you so many diamonds you won't need them any more.

FEVVERS: No. Don't. Stand back a bit. I want to breathe.

There is a struggle during which FEVVERS' dagger falls to the floor.

MR SUGAR: What's this?

FEVVERS: Nothing. It's from the old place. It's nothing.

MR SUGAR: It's very sharp. That's handy.

FEVVERS: How many diamonds could I have?

MR SUGAR: As many as you want. For as long as you want. Here – let me –

He starts to reach to the roots of the wings, making a space for the knife to cut.

FEVVERS: Wait.

MR SUGAR: I'm not a hard man. Bite on this while I'm cutting.

FEVVERS' words become inaudible as she is biting on the gag.

I think I can get behind the bone with the point. Are you ready?

FEVVERS grunts.

Ad lib. Just as he is about to cut, LIZZIE springs into the room like Zorro.

LIZZIE: Oh no you don't! I remember your type.

She beats him with the bag.

It's New Year's Eve, Mr Sugar. So goodbye to you. And to all those like you. Come on Fevvers.

She chucks her bag at him. He catches it. There is a mighty explosion.

ACT THREE

There is a long pause after the explosion. We are in a bare, white landscape.

COLONEL KEARNEY enters with his pig.

KEARNEY: Sybil.

Listen to me.

Everything is lost. The circus is blown up. All the animals dead. Buffo dead.

We might be the only ones left alive.

But hell! We won't let a little thing like this stop us.

We started with nothing and we will start with nothing again.

I throw down my challenge to the shooting stars – we will return with bigger and more ferocious tigers, with elephants.

Never say die? Eh Sybil.

Wake up Sybil. Wake up.

SAMSON enters with a pile of wood.

STRONG MAN: I make fire for you.

I have been too strong and too simple with my muscle.

I am sorry, the Mignon.

MIGNON: It's alright.

PRINCESS enters. She sees MIGNON.

PRINCESS: Mignon!

MIGNON: You can talk.

PRINCESS: I can talk as well as you can.
    I remained silent only for the sake of my cats.
    They hated the human voice
    As much as they loved my music.

    My father taught them to love music.
    My mother taught me to play.
    We have never been to Abyssinia.
    We are from Marseilles.

MIGNON: What is your name?

PRINCESS: Rhodora.

FEVVERS and LIZZIE enter.

FEVVERS: Jack! Jack!

LIZZIE: What do you want him for?

FEVVERS: I just want to know he's alright.

LIZZIE: And what are you going to do if we do find him?
    You know how it ends – misfortune is overcome, the
    lovers reunite – and then… Marriage.

FEVVERS: Marriage?

LIZZIE: Orlando takes his Rosalind. She says, 'To you I
    give myself, for I am yours.' And that goes for a girl's
    bank account, too.

FEVVERS: I'm not giving my bank account to anyone.

LIZZIE: That's my girl. Here's to the death of the happy
    ending!

FEVVERS: Oh but Liz – think of his soft look – as if you
    could mould him any way you want. Surely he'll have
    the decency to give himself to me, not the other way
    round. Let him hand himself over to me and I will
    transform him. You said he was unhatched, Lizzie. Well
    I'll sit on him. I'll hatch him out. I'll make a new man of

him – a fitting mate for the new woman, and we'll march onward hand in hand through the New Century.

LIZZIE: You don't know the first thing about the human heart. It is a treacherous organ and you're a greedy girl. Selling yourself is one thing – but chucking yourself out with the bath water is quiet another. What happens to that unique indivisible you, if you rashly throw yourself away? It falls to bits, that what happens to it. I raised you to fly up to the heavens, not brood over a clutch of eggs!

FEVVERS: You're jealous!

LIZZIE: I never thought I'd live to hear my girl say such a thing.

WALSER emerges from the white stuff where FEVVERS is sitting.

Oh gawd.

JACK: Fevvers.

You want to know what I want?

> I want to see you lying wherever you are lying
> Your hair caught in your fingers as you sleep
> I want to see your breath tickle the pillow
> Your fat cheek glowing hot against your wrist
>
> I want to hear you laughing as your eyes
> Wake up and start to eat another day.
> I want to listen to you sing, just once
> Without imagining a gilded cage.
>
> I want to feel the dark warmth of your body
> Rising like hands to hold me as I write.
> I want to taste the dry earth smell that drifts
> About you as you think and breathe and speak.

I want to feel each beat of life in you,
Each taste, each song, each joke, each fear, each
   dream.

LIZZIE has found a radio. She turns it on. It plays the music of Nina Simone.

JACK and FEVVERS fly.

VESTA: The laughter of the happy young woman rose up from the wilderness in a spiral and began to twist and shudder across the cold new world, as if a spontaneous response to the giant comedy that endlessly unfolded beneath it, until everything that lived and breathed, everywhere, was laughing.

Fevvers, sputtering to a stop at last, crouched above him, covering his face with kisses.

Oh how pleased with him she was!

Company sings 'Do You Know of the Land Where the Lemon Trees Grow?'

By the same authors

Kneehigh Anthology: Volume One
Tristan & Yseult / The Bacchae / The Wooden Frock / The Red Shoes
9781840025644

A Matter of Life and Death
9781840027815

WWW.OBERONBOOKS.COM

Follow us on www.twitter.com/@oberonbooks
& www.facebook.com/OberonBooksLondon